A Golf Guru!

by
Philip Rennett

FORE!

THE PRIME AIM of this book is not to make you a better golfer. You'll need a golf professional, new clubs, decades of practice, a different ball, other books, longer arms, a psychotherapist or a miracle to do that.

The aim of this book is to make you a golf guru. It will help you to get more out of the game. It will increase your enjoyment so that your last shot or your next shot are not the be-all-and-end-all of the round. You will walk off the course more regularly with a smile - not a grimace - on your face.

Once you achieve this, then you are indeed on your way to golfing enlightenment. And once you've started the journey, you will understand the lessons taught by the game that may actually help in the other, not-so-important aspects of your life, such as your marriage, your kids and your job.

Others will notice the change in your approach and the improvement in your demeanour. They will buy you drinks in the clubhouse, in the hope that you will pass on the secret of your newly found happiness, both on and off the course.

And you will share the lessons you have learned and the skills you have developed and which you continue to practice, for you are a golf guru and that's what gurus do.

Besides, you like free drinks.

First published in Great Britain in 2015
by Philip Rennett

Copyright © Philip Rennett 2015

All rights reserved.
This book or any portion thereof, in either printed or electronic form, may not be reproduced or used in any manner whatsoever without the express written permission of the publisher except for the use of brief quotations in a book review. Nor may it be otherwise circulated in any form of binding or cover other than that in which it is published without a similar condition being imposed on the subsequent purchaser.

Cover design by QSC

Printed by CreateSpace

Cover photo: Western Park Golf Club, Leicester

CONTENTS

Preface	9
Acknowledgements	13
Introduction	15
Why play golf?	19
Before the game begins	23
Teeing up success	27
There's no fair in fairway	35
The short route to victory	39
Finishing the hole	45
Halfway house	51
A good walk spoiled?	53
Mining verbal gold	55
Dressing for success	57
Better clubs better player?	59
Relying on the go-to club	61
Winning	65
Pressure	73
Lessons for life	79
The key points	101

PREFACE

HERE'S A QUESTION for golfers of all types and abilities. Why do you play golf?

Have you ever stopped to wonder why you spend a good proportion of your life trudging across fields in all kinds of weather, lugging a bag of metal sticks with you, trying to hit a small ball into a small hole, before taking it out and starting again? Or why you then do exactly the same thing the following week (or possibly sooner), probably on the same fields and (hopefully) using the same ball?

No? Me neither. Well, not until the Momentous Day.

It came on the seventeenth hole at Villamartin in Spain, halfway through a weeklong golfing break.

I had been playing poorly with only the occasional reminder why I was a half-decent golfer, and I couldn't seem to put a run of decent holes - or even decent shots - together.

The seventeenth hole is a 230-yard par 3 across a valley from an elevated tee, with a large, two-tier back-to-front sloping green and a high grass bank on the left hand side.

My tee shot sailed away with a touch of draw into a bright blue, cloudless sky and looked destined to hit the bank and roll gently onto the top level of the green where the flag happened to be.

In those lightning fast visions all golfers experience, I thought it could even trickle down to the hole and give me a good chance of a birdie.

A good chance, that is, until the only piece of vegetation on the bank – a small but bushy bush - got in the way of the ball's roll, leaving me a tricky stab shot downhill onto the fast surface, with plenty of green sloping away from the pin.

Resisting the temptation to sling my rescue wood into the nearest tree, or to change the club's lie forever by slamming it into the turf, or loudly cursing the golfing gods, I found myself shrugging my shoulders and, with half a smile on my face, declared "Well, that's golf for you."

My playing partners emerged from behind the buggy where they'd taken shelter from the anticipated flying club and the accompanying choice of loud and exotic swear words, their expressions ranging from puzzlement through to deep concern that they'd slipped into a parallel universe.

They had expected to confront a particularly nasty orc from Mordor, but what they got was a hobbit from the Shire – and a hobbit that had never ventured forth on any quest to do with a ring and was quite happy with his lot as a result.

I stared at the view in front of me, including the bushy bush, but I saw nothing. Despite my shoddy game, I realised that I was thoroughly enjoying the day and that one piece of spectacular misfortune wasn't going to spoil it. That thought shocked me so much that I don't remember the buggy drive down to the green and I barely recall the stab out and the two putts that followed.

Even today, it's tough to recall the look on my playing partner's face as his sixty-foot uphill putt from the front of the green made it up to the top level and almost into the hole before rolling sixty feet back down to him - a classic comedy moment.

Fortunately my memory recovered soon after, so I have a clear recollection of how good it felt responding to my moment of adversity with a calmness and serenity that would be the envy of the Dalai Lama himself.

Golf, it dawned on me, wasn't just a difficult and frustrating sport, or a battle against the elements or yourself. Neither was it just a competition you had to win, or something you did to have a laugh with your mates, or an excuse for a few post-round drinks.

There was much more to the sport than all those things combined. Golf was a teacher. A training ground for life. It was a live-fire exercise, designed to instill attitudes that would help the player to get the most out of their day-to-day existence, as well as their game.

The rest of my week was spent examining and analysing every reaction from my playing partners and myself to every shot on every course we played.

It did nothing for the quality of my game, which was shockingly bad, to be honest. But it gave me the idea for this book. I hope you get something out of it.

Phil Rennett
Spring 2015

ACKNOWLEDGEMENTS

WRITING A BOOK is very much like a game of golf, except it's you against the blank page rather than you against the course. And like golf, it's more fun if the writing process involves others.

In this case, there wouldn't be much of a book if it weren't for the people with whom I've had the pleasure to play. Stand up and take a bow Dol, Mark, Glen, Dave, Billy, Martyn, Clive, Deeve, Kev, Simon, Cockney Simon, Bolts, Pete, Bob, Ian, Alan, Gary, John, Mick and Paul. Apologies for any I've missed. I owe you a pint.

I'd also like to thank John Nicholls, who took the time to read through the original draft and to provide some useful feedback, despite his hectic schedule golfing and skiing near his home in Vancouver.

The best times I have had playing golf have been the occasional times my son Michael has joined me, proving what a natural he would be at this sport if he hadn't got better things to do with his time. Thanks pal!

Finally, I'd like to thank Clare for egging me on to get this book finished, for being incredibly supportive and for not going on too much about the time she hammered me twice on the putting green on Southwold sea front.

1. INTRODUCTION

DURING MY TIME on the golf course, I have seen Darth Vader, Happy Gilmore, the Dalai Lama, Ace Ventura, the Incredible Hulk, Eeyores by the dozen, Rocky and a whole host of other characters.

In other words, I've seen players elated, relieved, despondent, crushed, happy, phlegmatic, smug, malicious, amused, angry and depressed. We all have - possibly including someone so enraged you half expected them to turn green and turn their clothes to shreds.

I have feared for the health of playing partners, generally because their face was a peculiar shade of purple - either because they were so infuriated, or embarrassed, or out of breath, or because they were wetting themselves laughing at someone else's misfortune.

I have witnessed outstanding examples of sportsmanship, outrageous attempts at gamesmanship and outright violence.

But whatever I have seen, whatever I have been involved in, I have always followed one piece of sage advice I was given a number of years ago about any sport I played.

Always walk off with a positive. Whether it was a pass in football, a return in tennis, a tackle in rugby or a great bunker shot in golf, no matter what the result, walk off with that positive in mind. Admittedly, that can be a bit tricky if you've just missed a tiddler on the last for a win, but it is an edict I've always tried to follow – even if I sometimes have had to clutch tightly at a rather flimsy straw.

Let's face it: "At least my shoelaces didn't come undone" is not a rewarding memory after four hours of action.

Playing golf, the 'walk off with a positive' philosophy has sometimes been a tough one to remember, never mind follow. I haven't been able to pause for a second, take a step back, look at the bigger picture and – in doing so – get much more out of the game.

It boils down to this. Golf – like life - is so much better if you feel you're having a dozen good moments each day rather than a victory every now and then.

That's what this book is all about; providing ideas, thoughts and perspectives that will boost your enjoyment of the game, create a positive change in mindset that may impact on your scores, enhance your ability to recover more quickly from setbacks and - who knows - may even have benefits in your non-golfing life.

This isn't a golf-coaching manual. This is a golf experience manual. There are many better ways of learning how to cure your slice, spin your approach shot, splash out of sand or read a putt.

But once you've read this, I hope you'll get more out of the time you spend on the course. And the lessons you've learned could help you to get more out of your time off the course as well.

The book is split into two sections. In the first, we take a walk through the game – from pre-match preparation to sinking the final putt and everything in between. In the second, we look at other aspects of golf, which we can learn from and which we can use wherever we are and whatever we're doing.

By all means read the book from cover to cover, but feel free to dip in and out whenever and wherever you feel like. It's not a course with a diploma at the end. You won't remember all of it - although there is a helpful summary of the key points later on.

However, there will be thoughts and ideas that will strike a chord and that you'll take with you or that will come to mind the next time you venture forth in search of the perfect round.

Enjoy!

2. WHY PLAY GOLF?

WE WERE PLAYING in the first round of the club's major matchplay pairs' tournament. My partner – we'll call him Dan because that's his real name – had already been on the range for half an hour before I arrived at the club.

We chatted and joked while I warmed up and then we wandered over to the putting green and hit a few putts before meeting up with the rival pair – both good lads who we had played with once before.

It was a mild, sunny afternoon with a touch of light breeze. The group before us had driven off ten minutes earlier and there was nobody behind us on the tee. Conditions were perfect and all four of us managed to hit decent drives up and over the hill on the first.

On the green, Dan just missed an eight-footer for a par and the half - understandable when you're playing on our greens, which have more discrete borrows than a secret gambling addict.

"You're useless Jones!" Dan told himself. His self-beratement drowned out our muttered commiserations (we'd all suffered at the hands of that green at one time or another) and he stomped off to the second tee. We didn't know it at the time, but that hole was to be the highlight of the round. A

19

dark, seething cloud of anger had settled over Dan's head and nothing was going to shift it.

By the fifth hole, our rivals had decided that pleasant social chat wasn't going to help anybody and simply focused on their own game in an embarrassed silence, leaving me to try and raise the spirits of my increasingly despondent partner whilst battling to keep us hanging on to their coat tails.

By the ninth hole, Dan had run out of expletives to describe himself and his game and had drifted into a sullen silence, complemented by the occasional throwing and subsequent retrieval of a variety of clubs.

My efforts to raise his morale had worn me down as well and had affected my own game. We shook hands on the thirteenth, having lost seven and five. "I'm glad that's over," said Dan to nobody in particular but within earshot of all of us. None of us could disagree.

The winners declined to join us for a post-match drink. I think one had a royal wedding to attend and the other had a small nuclear device to disarm. So the two of us sat staring despondently at our beers, lost in our own worlds until I broke the silence.

"Why do you do it Dan? Why do you play golf?"

Dan took a gulp of his pint and put it back down on the table, watching the bubbles rise to the surface.

"I don't know," he said. He thought about it some more, finished his drink, bought a second, downed half of it in one and let out a discreet belch.

"I still don't know," he said. "Maybe I should give it up."

Several years later, Dan is still playing. In the intervening period, he's gone through a couple of relationships, a career change and has had heart problems.

He still beats himself up on the course every now and then, but not as much as before. He finishes almost every round now, rather than storming in after nine holes or even earlier. His game has improved slightly. His clubs rest easily in the bag rather than on the fairway, in ponds and up trees. He laughs more during the round.

A while back, we were in the clubhouse and were reminiscing about 'that' pairs game. I asked him the same question – why do you play golf. This time, there was more to the answer.

"To get some exercise and some fresh air; to see my mates; to wind down, have a laugh and to get away from the rest of my life; and to see if I can improve my game."

And what had changed since I first asked that question after the pairs disaster? The context.

"Then, it was all about wanting to win. Believing I was a better player than my handicap said I was; taking on shots I couldn't make and getting annoyed with myself when they didn't come off. Now, golf is an escape, a release. I just appreciate how lucky I am to be here, to be able to play and to use golf as a means of exercise and relaxation. I still get wound up, but I enjoy playing more."

Time and experience have certainly changed Dan's perspective for the better as far as golf is concerned, but we don't have to wait to go through such traumatic changes in our own personal circumstances in order to enhance our appreciation and enjoyment of the game.

And by consciously identifying what it is that makes the game so special to us - by recognising there is more to golf than hitting a small ball time and again into small holes across several fields - then we take more enjoyment out of every round; we increase the value of our time on the course; and we are more relaxed about the way we are playing.

Who knows, that change in attitude to the game could well result in an improvement in our scores. I thought about Dan's answer and realised I hadn't even considered the same question, so I did.

I wrote down a list of everything I liked about playing golf. Fresh air, 'me' time, great scenery, winning, the wind in what's left of my hair, occasional magical shots, sunshine on my back, bluebells in the woods and drives off elevated tees all made the cut.

Then I picked my top ten and memorised them. Every time I play, I see how many of my favourite things I can tick off my mental list. By doing so, I've built a greater appreciation of my time on the course and have managed to set the quality of my play in a broader, much more positive context.

3. BEFORE THE GAME BEGINS

SEVERAL YEARS AGO, twelve of us went on a week's golfing holiday in Spain, where we played six different courses around Fuengirola.

Every day, the first tee time was around 12.30 to give us time to recover from the (ahem) exertions of the previous evening. And every day, we ended up rushing into the pro shop about five minutes before our allotted time, then careering around like the Keystone Cops in six buggies, trying to find our first tee (which was sometimes the tenth).

For some unfathomable reason, I always seemed to be drawn in the first group. We'd race onto the tee muttering apologies to the starter, plonk down a ball, have two practice swipes as a warm up and then top one down the fairway or hook one into the rough.

Meanwhile, the rest of the group would at least have time for a gentle warm up and maybe a putt or two on a nearby practice green, while we hunted for our balls under the disdainful view of the starter.

The evening before our final game, I made an impassioned plea to the group. Could we at least get to the final course in plenty of time, so we could soak up the atmosphere, maybe grab a coffee, hit some balls on the range and get the feel of the greens with a reasonable number of practice putts. Everyone was in agreement.

We left earlier the next day (the hottest day of the holiday by far) and arrived one hour early, only to find the range was a time zone away, the putting green was being renovated and our buggies wouldn't be available until just before our first tee time.

The early start meant some of us were still suffering from mild hangovers and were desperate for a coffee or two to help us recover. Others had rushed out without picking up their bottles of cold water. We wandered over to the café, only to find it was closed as the lady who ran it had gone into town to pick up some ice.

We stood, huddled under what little shade was afforded by the small olive trees, watching other groups roll up from the range in their buggies, take a swig from their cold water bottles, wait their turn on the tee and then smash drive after powerful drive straight down the first fairway.

By the time our buggies turned up, vacated by a group of the most beautiful women I have ever seen on a golf course (they were Scandinavian), we were so red, tired and sweaty that not one of us even bothered to say hello.

Instead, we slumped into the seats, turned the buggy so we were in the shade of its roof and waited to be summoned to the tee, where our sweaty palms guaranteed yet another series of poor shots, to our chagrin and the piteous contempt of those who witnessed the start of our round.

The bitter irony of that day is still remembered by those who were there and has been used during the golf holidays of the intervening years as justification for the occasional last-minute arrival at the tee.

We all still see it today. Wherever you play, there will be people who turn up so late that they only realise where they are and what they're doing halfway down the third fairway.

Some lucky ones get away with it. And that's fine. It's part of their ritual and it works for them.

Maybe time spent on the range and the putting green would simply reinforce the faults in their game. Hanging around, soaking in the atmosphere and chatting to playing partners may heighten the tension and make them nervous. Having a pre-match coffee (or a beer or two - it has been known) could upset their equilibrium.

Maybe witnessing too many tee shots sailing away down the middle of the fairway builds pressure on their own start. Whatever the reasons behind their last-minute arrival, it's the way they like to start the game.

At the other end of the scale are those who arrive a couple of hours early and who spend most of that time warming up their bodies and ironing out any swing flaws on the range and the practice green.

They're the ones who have a bucket or two of balls and who never use the same club twice in succession – preferring instead to work their way around the course in their head. On the putting green, they use just the one ball, because you never get a second chance to putt from the same spot once you're on the course (air shots excepted).

Both forms of preparation and the hundreds of alternatives in between are more than acceptable if they work for you, but will cause others to scratch their heads in wonder if they don't work for them.

It goes to show that there are innumerable ways to get yourself ready for the challenges you face. You just have to find the one that's right for you and that puts you in a positive frame of mind for the game ahead.

Just as important as the physical preparation (or lack of it) is the mental preparation (or lack of it).

We've all seen players who have lost the game even before they've hit the first shot of the match. Then there are those people who are almost waiting for their first poor shot in order to give themselves a telling off and who then can't wait for the next one in order to increase the self-flagellation.

Others are unfailingly optimistic on the first tee, drawing on the success of a previous round and hoping to maintain or even improve on that standard - an aspiration that lasts until the first hook out of bounds or the three out of the bunker, when they slump into a slough of quiet despond.

There are those who are blessed with a calmness of mind, who accept poor shots, bad luck, superb strokes and outrageous fortune as part and parcel of the game and who walk off the eighteenth with the same demeanour they showed on the first.

Then there are the ones who can hit one great shot out of 114 and come off the course with a smile on their face, alongside the player who has hit one poor shot out of 76 and who walks off with a face like thunder.

Some stop caring. Others simply stop.

What a game, that reveals our true nature and exposes our very soul to all around, simply by hitting a ball around a field.

4. TEEING UP SUCCESS

THE TEE SHOT is a unique shot in the game of golf. It's the only shot over which – in theory – you have total control.

You decide how your ball is to sit. You choose, within fairly generous limits, where to place it. The ball is even set up on a tee to make sure the strike is nice and clean.

Apart from the occasional breeze, nothing affects your stance or your swing. And nobody has an advantage over you in terms of ball position on the course.

All you need to do is to decide on the right shot, select the right club and hit the ball as planned. It's as simple as that. Honestly. Except it isn't, is it?

Some time ago, a group of us played the Brabazon course at The Belfry. That's the beauty of golf. If you can scrape together the cash, you can play where the world's best have played.

After the group in front of us had left the first tee, we wandered on to have a look at the fairway and to soak in the atmosphere. The starter welcomed us and gave us a brief pep talk on what to expect.

"As you can see gents, that long bunker means all the trouble is down the left hand side of the hole. The wind will be coming over your left shoulder. The best play is a rescue club or a long iron into the middle of the fairway and then a medium to long iron into the heart of the green."

We all nodded sagely, thanked him for his advice, walked over to our golf bags and returned, slightly sheepishly, each with a driver in hand. He smiled knowingly (and a little wearily) and courteously wished us a good game.

Miraculously, given the pressure we had put ourselves under with the decision to go big, we all got our tee shots away successfully and walked off the tee nice and calmly, as professionals would do, before spoiling the image by giggling between ourselves once we reached our trolleys.

Forget course management. To the vast majority of golfers out there, tee shots are all about getting the ball as close to the hole as possible. Laying up is something you do when you have a bad back or a bad leg and there's sport on the television.

On par threes, you want to be on the green and will select an iron or a wood that you think will get you there in one. On par fours and fives, it's simply a matter of belting the ball as far down the fairway as you possibly can.

That means getting out your driver - the Big Dog, the most macho club in the bag - and unleashing a swing so fluid and powerful that the ball burns the air during its flight, screaming over the course and the admiring golfers below before gravity finally catches up and drags it gracefully back to earth and onto the lush green fairway 300-plus yards away.

And then you wake from your reverie to find yourself staring at the ball you've just teed up, the driver face waiting patiently behind it and your playing partners watching expectantly. How do you feel now? Confident? Or do you feel nervous? Are you worried about what may happen next? And if so, how do you overcome those negatives?

I have a friend who would be a decent golfer if he could stop thinking negatively whenever he steps on the course.

When the occasional miracle occurs and he's putting a good round together and threatening to win the money, there's a very easy way to ensure the latter doesn't happen.

When he's walking onto the tee, simply say to him: "I reckon this is going to be a great shot." Invariably, his answer is: "I doubt it." and guess what, it isn't.

That's not to say the opposite would happen if he changed the habit of a lifetime and agreed with me, but it does show how important that final swing thought can be.

On the par five eighth at my own club, the view from the raised tee includes 100 yards or so of downhill heavy rough leading to a large stream that crosses in front of the uphill fairway, which is flanked by trees on the right hand side and an out-of-bounds farmer's field on the left.

The wind is rarely with you on this exposed hole and can make a significant impact on the direction and flight of any tee shot.

In the seven years I've played there, my tee shots have meant I've developed a detailed - some would say intimate - knowledge of the trees on the right hand side. I'm only on nodding terms with the fairway.

In the first round of last year's club championship (a two-round medal competition for very good players and masochists only), I did something I had never done before.

Having arrived at the eighth tee three shots over par, I pulled my drive straight into the farmer's field, much to the consternation of the sheep, who had been doing their best to put me off with their incessant bleating.

I put down another ball, aimed at my favourite tree on the right and still managed to hook this second ball into the same field on the left.

The sheep wondered what the hell was going on and so did I. Out came the four iron and, a mere seven shots later, I walked away from the green with my confidence shot to pieces – still with ten holes to play and another full round the next day.

Arriving at the clubhouse the next day, I had already determined to use an iron on the eighth tee and to leave my driver in the bag.

By the time I reached the site of the previous day's nightmare however, I had hit three very reasonable drives and my confidence in the Big Dog has returned. That confidence lasted fifteen seconds.

The sheep must have known what was coming. They made no sound and had scurried to the top left corner of their field, as far out of range as possible, where they looked on with the mild curiosity they probably display when the farmer turns up with his trailer to select and to take away some who mysteriously never return...

Standing over the ball, the memories of the previous day came flooding back. Canute-like, I strove to repel them by thinking of the great drives I had hit since then. I swung the club; the ball sailed off into the blue yonder. I never took my eyes off it. Not until it disappeared behind the bushes that masked the farmer's field.

It was only after I had hit my second ball the same way

that I realised what the final swing thought had been for each of my tee shots on the hole that weekend.

Whatever you do, don't hit it left.

Negative thoughts don't make good swing thoughts.

So much of the golf swing involves body mechanics that are governed by the brain. Negative thoughts cause the brain to react cautiously and defensively, affecting the natural swing and resulting in an unnatural shot. Such shots never go where you want them to go. They cause you to lose confidence in your swing, which affects your ability to play the game.

If you're not careful, you're in a downward spiral that can be tricky and time consuming to reverse.

Maybe it was the pressure of the event – the biggest of the year and an 'every shot counts' medal to boot. I hoped that was the case and, as it turned out, I haven't been anywhere near that field since. The trees on the right have welcomed me back with open branches.

It's strange how using the same club can have such different results on different holes. I know I can use my driver to hit the ball straight down the middle on our first. I can use the same club to draw the ball around the corner on our second. I can hit it straight or with a slight fade depending on the tee position on the sixth.

I don't even think about where the ball is going, never mind worry about it, but stepping onto that eighth tee niggles away at my confidence.

I counter it with a recent memory. Looking down at the ball, I imagine I'm back on the sixth tee and swing accordingly.

The results aren't perfect (as the trees continue to testify), but each tee shot that doesn't finish up a sheep's backside pushes the horrors of the club championship further into the recesses of my memory and helps to rebuild my confidence on the hole.

The best way to maintain confidence on the tee is to hit a club that you know will keep you in play, even if that means leaving the Big Dog in the kennel.

Crashing the ball into trees 230 yards away or keeping the ball in the fairway 20 yards further back with a shot to the green – which would you prefer?

And yet, many of us still pull out the driver because there is a secret on the tee that we men (and occasionally women) are aware of, but very rarely discuss unless something unusual happens.

Distance off the tee is a rather sad and inaccurate reflection of our manhood. *See how far he hits the ball; truly he is a man among men, even if it has flown into that farmer's yard and out of bounds.*

Yet the only time this is openly discussed is when one of the weaklings amongst us manages to hit a decent drive down the fairway and - miracle of miracles - is not the first to hit their second shot.

"Look. He's outdriven Dave." Mild gloating, then a frisson of palpable tension crackles for a moment as the group contemplates what that means. The old order has been toppled. The king is dead; long live the king – a feeling that lasts until the usurper tops his second shot, or slices his tee shot on the next hole and the natural order is restored.

Here's an idea. It's a big ask but, on your next social round, leave your driver and your machismo in your car and

32

try teeing off with another club or two on the par fours and fives instead.

Check where you finish compared to your driver in terms of distance and accuracy and see if the change has any impact on your score.

If the outcome is positive, then you have plenty of options on the tee, neatly sidestep the machismo competition and have a great line for those who may mock your decision to leave the driver in the bag.

"Nah. Don't need it."

5. THERE'S NO FAIR IN FAIRWAY

A FAIRWAY IS such an ironic description of that piece of land between the tee and the green. Hitting the fairway from the tee is only the first of the challenges you face on each hole (par threes excepted). Many of those challenges are a consequence of that original shot and, if golf teaches us one thing about life, this is the biggest lesson of the lot.

Golf - like life - isn't fair.

You can hit the best drive of your life off the tee, launching the ball into the wild blue yonder to see it fall gracefully into the middle of the short grass you were aiming for and yet, and yet…

A nasty bounce off a slope or a sprinkler head can push you into trees or a hazard. On some holes, created by miserable people who hated life, were bullied at school and who never had sex, a straight drive into the middle of a straight fairway will leave a massive oak tree between you and the green.

Divots have their own special role to play in making a golfer's life a misery. They turn smiles of satisfaction following a tremendous tee shot into worried frowns or wails of despair depending on your overall emotional state and, more than likely, a hail of expletives directed at the idiot who decided not to repair their divot but simply walk past the recently-excavated turf whilst admiring their shot.

As mentioned before, your local pro is a far better reference point when it comes to hitting 165 yards from a divot, snap hooking around the tree or punching a fade out of the copse.

What this book is about is making sure you are in the right frame of mind to execute whatever shot is required.

That involves three things – laughter, the ability to put things in context and a positive, albeit realistic, mindset.

Let's face it. We have slices of misfortune on the fairway, but we also have slices of luck when an errant tee shot heading for a neighbouring field or a dark, dense wood bounces back into play, courtesy of the same trees or slopes we now curse. It's just that we forget when fortune has been in our favour.

The course giveth and the course taketh away. Remembering this with a smile in our time of misfortune will help us to accept our lot this time around and will ensure we approach the recovery shot with blood pressure and adrenaline levels much lower than they would otherwise be and with a calmness that will enable us to focus effectively on the next inevitable challenge rather than fuming over the last one.

Find the extraordinary in the ordinary

One of my favourite off-course activities is to remember my greatest shots from my most recent game. In fact, I'm starting to relish these as I walk off the course – but I don't talk about them in the clubhouse at the end of the round unless someone else brings them up (although the context tends to be "What about your fluked pitch on the fifth?" - which isn't quite how I saw it at the time or afterwards).

These are not necessarily match-winning putts or huge drives. They're just the shots that give me most pleasure, reinforce my belief that I can still play this game well occasionally and boost my desire to get back on the tee as soon as decently possible.

Most of them occur on the fairway and most of the ones that occur on the fairway happen when I'm in trouble – which is why, although I don't look for problems, I relish the chance to get out of them. That doesn't mean looking for a miracle shot. It means trying something imaginative and well thought out, or attempting a shot you've been practicing and seeing it pay off.

I try to turn the problem into an opportunity to create something memorable. Sometimes, the only option is to chip out, or to take a drop. If that's the only thing you can do, then that's what you do. There'll be times down the line where the bounce will be in your favour once more. And there'll certainly be plenty of chances to find the extraordinary in the ordinary.

Leave machismo in the bag

Sadly, the machismo competition isn't confined to the tee area. It rears its head on the fairway as well.

"You've got 150 to the front of the green. What are you taking? A wedge?"

You stand near your bag, seven iron in hand. You show him the number on the iron (for the pedants, this is a social game) and tolerate his surprised expression and the raised eyebrows.

The key is to ignore the peer pressure. Nobody knows your game better than you. Your job is to get your ball safely on the green and into the hole.

And if that fool wants to end up short or in the bunker, then that's his prerogative.

Thinking about it, for some players, this game is all about ego. Longer than you, higher than you, closer than you, better than you and so on. Pity them, for they have mental issues and deserve your sympathy.

Golf, after all, is just a game. It's about enjoying yourself, relishing the challenges and your achievement in overcoming them (or at least some of them) and creating warm memories to keep you going until the next time you head out onto the course.

6. THE SHORT ROUTE TO VICTORY

DESPITE THE YEARS we sacrifice and the thousands of miles we walk, the vast majority of us will never be professional golfers and will struggle to possess a single-figure handicap.

We don't hit the ball far enough. We lack pinpoint accuracy off the tee and, as a result, we're too good at finding hazards and other obstacles – both physical and mental.

However, there is one area on every hole where you can match the pros and your club's A-team for distance and that's from 100 yards in to the green.

Even when we're old, or decrepit, or simply very hung over from the night before, hitting a golf ball over that kind of distance should not be beyond us.

If we are willing to put in the time and effort on the range and if we are willing to invest if necessary in a little coaching, there's no reason why we can't knock a few shots off our scorecard simply by flighting the ball over whatever is in its path and onto the green – allowing it to gaze down contemptuously at the hazards it has successfully avoided as it sails over them.

Just imagine how much more enjoyable golf would be if we didn't hook approaches into the water, fluff flop shots into the bunker, take two or more to get out of the sand or blade chip shots into the bushes at the back of the green.

How fantastically boring would it be if every shot from 100 yards in ended with the satisfying 'plop' of the ball landing gently a reasonably short distance from, or at least on the same playing surface as, the pin. And it's within our grasp!

There, lecture over… apart from to note that there's as much joy in hitting a great approach shot that avoids these hazards as there can be in matchplay when you see your opponent succumb to their attraction.

Even as you commiserate in the latter circumstances, your heart leaps a little and you think "Yes!" in your head. Just make sure it stays in your head though. The rest of the round can be quite strained if you actually say it out loud.

Ironically, this area of the course tends to be the most picturesque; the sand bunkers, the humps and hollows, the trees and the bushes, the bubbling stream and the occasional languid pool, all surrounding an immaculate, well-defined piece of turf and the slender flag pole. (I used 'hollow' rather than 'swale' as the definition of the latter is "a shallow depression on a golf course" and we all know that depression on a golf course is rarely shallow.)

Like the Lorelei of Germanic legend whose singing lured the river boatmen of the Rhine to destruction on a reef, these scenes of natural beauty conceal in full view an array of obstacles that can destroy a decent round.

Playing in Spain on a course where buggies had to stay on the path, I found myself chauffeuring a fair weather, bang-crash-wallop golfing pal whose second tee shot on the short par-4 first had landed in bushes to the left of the fairway.

He had managed to shank his first tee shot out of bounds onto the balcony of the clubhouse and was still recovering from the embarrassment.

Having found his ball with a direct route to the green blocked, he took a few deep breaths, decided not to play a 90-degree snap hook and knocked the ball thirty yards out onto the fairway.

He then wandered out to his ball to decide on his next shot. I forgave him for not taking any clubs as I was impressed, if not a little amazed, to see the thought he was giving to the hole.

He wandered back to the buggy and rummaged in his bag before starting off to his ball again. "What are you taking?" I asked, thinking a seven or eight iron would be about right.

"My camera," came the reply. "It's a lovely view."

Having taken his photograph – and acutely aware from the oaths and insults floating over the course towards him that other members of the group were still waiting to start their round - he trotted back to the buggy.

"What shall I take?" he asked.

"How should I know?" I replied, "You've been out there twice already; surely you've got some idea?"

He grabbed a nine iron, ran back to his ball and topped it into the stream crossing the fairway twenty yards further on. He walked quickly up to the stream, retrieved his ball and, still using the nine iron, bladed it into a greenside bunker before returning to the buggy sweating profusely.

I suppose I was expecting some form of shame-faced half-apology, half-explanation.

"Well," he said, "What a lovely view…"

It is fine - indeed, it is desirable - to recognise and appreciate the beauty of a golf course. It's all part of the game. It's one of the joys of playing and can be a comfort if you're not playing well.

But there has to be a time and a place for such appreciation. Otherwise, why would you bother lugging a bag of clubs around with you? You'd be better off going for a walk instead.

Splashing out

What strikes the most fear into a golfer - sand or water? It's probable that we see more sand on a course than we do water. Bunkers may appear on virtually every hole; water rarely features as often but makes a bigger target. But does familiarity make us more or less fearful?

Talking to a number of players of varying ability, the consensus was that water is nice to look at and fairly easy to avoid unless you're playing a ball that is strangely attracted to it.

The downside is that water costs you balls as well as shots. I should know. The first time I played Laguna (the clue's in the name) in the Algarve, I lost ten balls on four holes, each of which featured water.

At the same time, there are very capable golfers whose legs turn to jelly if they land in a bunker or if one is on their line to the pin.

We'll all have stories of low handicappers taking seven to get out of sand in a medal and we'll all have chunked chip shots into sand at one time or another, when the green on the other side was easy to reach.

Sand gets in your head. The best way of getting out is peddled in all kinds of media and goes totally against the (ahem) grain of every other shot you take: open the clubface, aim to the left of the pin (which confuses left handers), dig your feet in and don't hit the ball.

There will be times when this works; there will be others when it doesn't and the ball will remain obstinately close to where you stand or will sail out of bounds on the other side of the green.

Most of the time, failing to extricate yourself first time is down to you. Occasionally, the ball's position makes an immediate escape extremely difficult, if not downright impossible but hey, you put the ball there in the first place.

What you can't beat however, is the feeling you get when you miraculously play this shot to perfection, watching the ball sail through a storm of sand to land safely on the green with a touch of check and then a graceful roll to a halt next to or inside the hole.

That, my friends, is a shot of genius and wonder. It's one to savour over the post-game pint, during the drive home and over the working week. The next time you're in a bunker, that shot could be yours.

Focus on the flag

Walking up to your approach shot, it's inevitable that you pay attention to the sand and water in your line of vision.

It's likely that your thought process will focus on the negatives - don't hit it short, don't hook it left, don't push it etc. – and you'll be subconsciously envisioning the problems you'll face if you make that kind of error. What you need to do is to turn melodrama into mellow drama!

Walking up to your approach shot, keep your focus on the flag and the green. Imagine your shot sailing into the air and landing on the green; imagine it again, then once more. Then stand over your ball and hit it.

It'll be interesting to see if focusing on positive images just before the strike has a positive impact on the results of the shot. If it doesn't work and you find yourself in the nearby hazard, relish the opportunity to create a memorable moment for yourself with the recovery shot. Remember: make the extraordinary from the ordinary!

7. FINISHING THE HOLE

FOR EVERY OTHER shot on the course, you have a choice of club. If the driver's not going well, you drop to a three wood or a low iron. Going under the ball with your lob wedge? Pull out your sand iron. But on the green, you only use the one club. And it has to work.

It's responsible for around 36 shots each round – almost as many as all the other clubs in your bag combined. It can turn a reasonable round into a nightmare or a good round into a great one.

It's the hole finisher (unless you've been extremely lucky); the match winner; the game breaker; the confidence booster; the mind scrambler; the nerves revealer.

The putter. The most used, and probably the least practiced, club in the bag.

The variety of designs is vast – each one intended to compensate for a weakness in your stroke or to make a good stroke more consistent.

Some look plain ugly; others are just plain, functional pieces of metal. Some wouldn't look out of place as branding irons on a cattle ranch or as a model for a space ship in Star Wars; others just look gorgeous. All have one role in life, to knock a ball into a hole.

The range of options is a fair indication of the number of ways a putt can be hit and reflects the predisposition of the golfer to blame the club rather than themselves for any weakness on the green.

Guilty as charged, I have six putters, collected during times of crisis over the last twenty years or so.

Unlike other clubs, which have come and gone and now reside in someone else's bag or lie forgotten and festooned by cobwebs in the dark recesses of the garage, I never get rid of my putters and they're always close to hand, just in case.

It's funny how you can fall in and out of love with your putter. When it's hot, you adore it. Confidence surges through you whenever you take it out of the bag. It's your best friend; it's an extension of your very being – you are as one. And then you miss a tiddler.

You put the first miss down to being one of those things – after all, you can't hole them all. But then you miss a second and the doubts start to niggle away.

From then on, it's as if you suspect your partner's cheating on you and you keep looking for confirmation. Each time you take the putter out of the bag, you're looking for signs of infidelity and, strangely, the more you look, the more you find.

You think "It must be me", but you're still hitting the ball the way you've always hit the ball, reading line and length as well as ever. The ball just refuses to drop, preferring instead to trundle well past the hole or stopping annoyingly short, leaving treacherous tap-ins that somehow lip out more often than they used to.

We've already established it's not down to you, and it'd be

ridiculous to blame an inanimate object like the ball. No, it all comes down to the traitorous putter.

"Maybe it's time for a change," you think. "Time for a fresh start."

Having flirted with a few replacements in the pro shop and eventually being seduced into spending wads of cash on a new blade, you dump your faltering old friend and embark on a new and exciting relationship.

But there's still a deep-down affection for your ex. You still remember the good times and think there may be a time in the future when the old flame could be rekindled. So your old putter is exiled to the cupboard where it waits patiently until you see the error of your ways, regret the break-up and ask for a second, or third, or fourth chance.

In our heart of hearts, we know it's not the putter that's to blame. I remember three-putting from six feet one time and, as I finally picked the ball out of the hole, my playing partner informed me there was 'some crap' at the end of my club. I lifted it up to inspect the blade only to be told, "No. The other end."

He had a point.

After all, the putt is the easiest shot to grasp in golf. Want proof? Just take your non-playing partner down to the range some time and get them to hit some irons and some woods. It's funny to watch. Air shots, tops and slices abound. Managing to get anything off the ground is a victory. Landing within forty yards of the target is a rare bonus.

Now get them on the putting green and ask them to hit some putts. In fact, make it a competition between you, watch them kick your ass and be prepared for their victory to be brought up *ad nauseum* for the foreseeable future and beyond.

Okay, not every putt will be perfect, but they'll hit every shot without feeling any pressure or with any great expectation of it going in. And there's the rub. The better we think we are, the greater the expectation.

The more we expect to hole out, the bigger the pressure on us to do just that.

The consequent physical and mental impact of that responsibility invariably leads to over-thinking the line or trying too hard to achieve the required length. The result? A miss, which adds to the pressure the next time around.

The fact is, we expect too much of ourselves. Even the pros don't sink everything and they are putting on a quality of surface we very rarely enjoy. Taking a rough average of the myriad of statistics quoted online, pros miss around one-fifth of their six-footers, half of their eight-footers and two-thirds of putts between ten and 15 feet. So why do we expect to do better, or get anywhere close to those figures?

I recently played in a foursomes where my playing partner asked me to try and leave my approaches more than five feet away from the pin, to give him a chance of holing the putt.

I often left him much, much further away than the requested minimum and he was in his element, sinking the putts from 15 feet and more, or at least leaving me with a tap in. But the couple of times I transgressed and left him within a yard, he turned to jelly and missed by a mile.

He thought every putt within that distance should drop and the pressure of expectation affected his swing. From further out, he was easier on himself, believing anything ending in gimme range was acceptable. As a result, the tension in him dissipated, the stroke remained true and we benefited from some excellent pars and a couple of birdies.

We put pressure on ourselves in all sorts of different ways.

In the same round, I bottled it when I saw my partner wandering up to the green without his putter, expecting me to sink a three-footer of my own. I was already imagining him stomping back to his bag before my ball had even lipped out.

Two words that strike fear into my own heart tend to be uttered during betterball or am-am competitions, when a score has already been set on a hole by your team but you have the opportunity to go one better and, in an attempt to encourage you, somebody utters, "Free roll."

In other words, "No pressure. We've already got points on the board so have a crack at it mate."

Unfortunately, what I hear is, "We have already done our bit Phil and have worked hard to secure points on this hole for our team. Our labours have resulted in you having a risk-free opportunity to build on our platform and now we expect you to take advantage of that and thereby enhance our chances of winning the competition by sinking this pressure-free putt."

So how do we rid ourselves of this pressure? How do we make sure we give ourselves the best possible chance of success on the green?

You may have noticed that this isn't a coaching manual. I've told you enough times. Believe me, you really wouldn't want me as your coach.

Your local pro is the best bet, followed by practice, practice and more practice. You'll end up with a more consistent, technically proficient swing and a greater ability to read a line and distance.

Knocking the ball into the hole time and time again will help build your confidence and will positively influence your mindset once you're on the course. Positively influence, mind you – not alter forever.

There will still be the times when the ball doesn't drop; when the pressure starts to build; when the mind games with your playing partners begin or when the magic words are uttered - "Free roll."

This is when you need to have a phrase in your head that acts like a valve, releasing all the negative thoughts and their physical manifestations (tighter grip, quicker follow through, jerky pick up etc.).

You need a couple of words that prompt you to remember that this is, after all, a game to be relished and enjoyed; a simple thought that replaces all the mental clutter with a clearness and a calmness of mind, where the only thing that matters is a steady swing and a good contact, followed by a comforting and rewarding plop as the ball hits the bottom of the cup.

I find "Sod it" works quite well.

8. HALFWAY HOUSE

SO, THERE WE have it. We've walked the course and have looked at every kind of shot you could face. But that's only half the story. We now turn our attention to other facets of the great game of golf.

And then we look at how this fantastic sport can provide us with useful lessons for life, helping each and every one of us to become a better person and, at the same time, providing us with even greater justification for spending more time on the course.

9. A GOOD WALK SPOILED?

THE DEFINITION OF golf as 'a good walk spoiled' couldn't be further from the truth. Golf isn't a good walk; it's a series of stutters.

It's a stroll broken up by innumerable halts - sometimes only after a handful of yards - as you look for balls or wait for your partners to play their shots.

Certainly, if you can drag your focus away from your ball for a moment, the views can be spectacular and the delays mean there's plenty of time to take them in.

Those same delays also ensure that gasping for breath, hot sweats and burning muscles are nowhere near as prevalent as they would be on a yomp up your nearest hill.

Golf, therefore, offers the opportunity to stretch your legs in the fresh air, with plenty of rest stops that can be used to take in the beauty of your surroundings.

There are quite a few 'good walks' I've been on that I would like to have had spoiled in that manner.

That isn't to say that walking around the course offers no physical challenge. A number of clubs have at least one incline known affectionately as 'heart attack hill' and there's always a member around to tell you the story of some poor soul who gasped his last breath on that very slope.

And if you're carrying, pushing or pulling your clubs around a course softened by the rains of a British winter (or summer for that matter), then you'll feel the results of your exertions the minute you try to get up and walk after an hour relaxing in the clubhouse.

Only the fittest amongst us can manage that particular exit without walking like an extra in a John Wayne western.

10. MINING VERBAL GOLD

A WALK AROUND a golf course also offers the opportunity for excellent conversation and banter - something that can prove impossible as you struggle to suck in life-sustaining air with a rucksack on your back, halfway up Ben Nevis.

Four hours gives you plenty of time to exchange news, swap local gossip, review recent sport results and generally put the world to rights.

It also allows for plenty of gaffes - verbal gold that can be enjoyed at the time, recounted in the clubhouse and then revisited for years afterwards to raise a chuckle and to embarrass the originator.

In recent times, members of my regular golfing group have discussed the attributes of many golf pros including Sam Tolerance, Bubble Watson and Ian Poultice.

Who knew that it was legless World War Two fighter ace Douglas Bader who founded the Scouts movement?

Just after the end of London 2012, we were encouraged to recognise the superb performance of our athletes in the Paramedics.

Enjoying a fine, hot day on the course, we have been advised to apply generous quantities of sun scream. And we have learned that a more descriptive term for the semi-rough is the long short grass.

Battling through a hailstorm, we've been comforted by the notion that "At least the rain is dry."

On top of these entertaining errors, certain individuals confuse their left with their right, resulting in near carnage when wayward shots have been followed immediately by a shout of "Fore left! No... right! No... left!"

To rectify this problem, one particular friend has a large L written on his white golf glove to remind him which side is which. The only problem is the time it takes for him to hold both hands out in front of himself after his shot, in order to verify the direction of the ball.

It's funny, but we've taken to shouting on his behalf instead. Just in case.

11. DRESSING FOR SUCCESS

THE LATE, GREAT Robin Williams used to say that golf was the only sport that gave a man the opportunity to dress like a pimp and nobody would care.

Of course, style is very much a personal choice, but looking at some of the fashion nightmares that pass for golf wear, he had a point. Some players clash so grievously with the natural hues of a golf course, there's an argument they should be penalised a shot per hole.

The stars of our game can get away with the look – firstly because they have a team of stylists and designers to ensure they are at least colour coordinated; secondly because they have the game needed to justify the attention they call to themselves. It's the latter where most of us fall down.

Wearing a red Nike golf shirt, or psychedelic clown trousers or some natty calfskin shoes doesn't make us Tiger Woods or John Daly or Miguel Angel Jimenez. It justifies the marketing and sponsorship strategies of the manufacturers.

It means the wearer attracts attention around the golf club, receiving admiring glances, contemptuous looks and verbal ridicule in equal measure – not that they care necessarily. Dressing like their hero inspires their game; puts them in the zone; helps them to focus. They believe they thrive under the pressure they place on themselves.

While many golfers are happy to play under a cloak of relative anonymity as they walk the fairways, doing battle with the course and their game without undue distraction, the 'affashionados' deliberately call attention to themselves and every shot they play.

"Look at me," they say subconsciously. "See how I master the intricacies of this course and the complexities of this sport. Marvel at my confidence as I stroll with a laconic gait up the middle of each fairway, or into the middle of each green without so much as a glance at the hazards that abound and threaten the very sanity of lesser mortals." At least, that's what some of them say – and fair play to them.

To others, there is a misguided logic to their choice of clothing and footwear. "Ian Poulter plays great golf and wears Union Jack trousers. Therefore, if I wear Union Jack trousers, I will play great golf." Oh dear.

You can easily identify the poor fools who follow this logic. They're the ones dressed like Blackpool illuminations, hacking their ball from tee to green, staring at their club as if they've never seen one before, climbing out of bunkers or searching in the long stuff, dirtying their outfit as they do so.

So, which are you? If you spend more time contemplating your outfit for the day than you do a round's worth of putts, then you dress for success and good luck to you. If you look good, you feel good and if, when you feel good, it's reflected in your game, then all is right with the world.

If your investment in your wardrobe isn't being justified on the course however, then perhaps it's time to spend your clothing budget on lessons instead.

12. BETTER CLUBS BETTER PLAYER?

I THINK WE'D all agree that what you have in your golf bag is more important than what you wear.

Playing to the best of your ability means a number of things have to fall into place. Certainly, that means being comfortable in your clothes and shoes, but it also means being happy with the clubs you use and the balls you hit. And this doesn't mean you have to use the latest technologies and the most expensive equipment.

Most golfers would be happy to use a driver and fairway woods that make the ball travel an acceptable distance in the direction they're aiming, plus a set of irons that will enable them to hit the ball well across a range of distances.

As Dirty Harry put it so memorably, "A man's got to know his limitations."

"None the more so," Clint Eastwood's character may have added, "Than when playing golf."

I've been told by many a pro that it really doesn't matter how far you can hit a particular club, just as long as (a) you know how far that distance is and (b) you can use different clubs to hit the ball different distances.

As an example, my pitching wedge will travel 110 yards, my nine iron 125, my eight 140 and my seven iron 155 yards.

Those were the distances I was hitting 25 years ago with my first set of Ben Sayers golf clubs and I'm hitting similar distances now with my set of second-hand Pings.

There are golfers out there who struggle to achieve any more distance with one iron than they do with another. Then there are others who defy the conventions of golf club design by hitting the ball further with one club than they do with another designed to achieve a greater distance.

We're all different, and so will be our weapons of choice. Just find some you feel comfortable with, that are nice to swing and that help you to hit the ball consistently to a range of distances. That's all you need.

What will happen is that, as your game improves and your scores start to drop, you look at how to take your game to the next level. The more sensible among us will realise this entails more practice; adding some finesse to your game; learning how to play different shots; improving your course management and thereby improving your shot selection.

The vast majority of us, however, reason that to be better players, we need better kit. There is some value in that rationalisation and the likes of Ping, Titleist and so on rely on it to stay in business.

It's certainly easier to hit drives straighter today than it was a couple of decades ago. And while not convinced that I need to be using ProV1s in order to improve my game, you won't catch me using balls of a perceived average quality either.

13. RELYING ON THE GO-TO CLUB

IT'S AMAZING HOW fragile a golfer's confidence can be. Equally amazing is the ability of golfers to travel through time. And both happen to be related.

No matter how good a golfer is, they didn't start that way. Everyone has had their fair share of shanks, hooks, duffs and (horror of horrors) air shots as they learn about the game and develop their swing.

Gradually, a style begins to form; confidence grows. Usually, the latter starts with a 'go-to' club; one item in your bag that you notice you're using slightly better than anything else.

For Alfie, it was a six iron. When he swung that club, the ball would fly straight and true. Once the ball was in play, his first thought would be "Can I use my six iron?" And if he could, he would.

The rest of his game was, if we're being generous, very average, but time and again his six iron would get him out of trouble and keep him competitive. He did use his other clubs occasionally, to stop them from feeling lonely, avoid accusations of neglect and basically to justify buying them in the first place, but in truth he was always looking for an excuse to revert to his beloved.

Many readers are smiling knowingly at this moment. We all know what happens next.

Favourite clubs never remain favourite clubs and the *denouement* is never pretty.

In Alfie's case, it happened on the seventeenth hole at Hanbury Manor, during his second round on the course in two days. For 34 consecutive holes, his six iron had worked like a dream – so much so, he'd only used five clubs during the whole of the second round.

That was about to change on the seventeenth – a twisting par five with a small lake front right of the green. Alfie's duffed tee shot followed by a six iron left him with 170 yards to the pin.

The shot was a challenge. Alfie normally hits a good six iron about 160 yards, but he was playing well and fancied his chances of making at least a par. Two practice swings and the ball was on its way, looking for all the world as if it would drop next to the pin. Looking for all the world, that is, until the splash. The big splash. The "Look, you're not even near the green-side bank, you hacker!" splash.

Without a word, he took another ball from his pocket and dropped it on the fairway. Before we could say anything, the second ball was on its way, with exactly the same results.

Alfie reached for another ball. "Remember you can take a drop anywhere on the line," someone pointed out. "Take a drop a bit closer to the green." The rest of us didn't bother. We'd seen the look before.

Alfie couldn't believe his go-to club had let him down. He was determined to demonstrate his faith in the iron wasn't misplaced and that meant proving it would help him to hit the shot he wanted to hit. Two more balls ended in a watery grave. "That's me done," he said, "I've no balls left."

The silence was deafening. We had witnessed Alfie's own Tin Cup moment and none of us knew what to say. We'd like to think we'd have done things differently, but we had all had our own special clubs and we knew how it felt to have that implicit faith destroyed in the space of one or two errant swings.

As we develop as golfers, we become more proficient with a wider selection of our clubs, but we are still prone to time travel every now and then.

An inexplicable shank will rudely halt a series of dozens, if not hundreds, of perfectly acceptable shots with a particular club.

If we're not careful, this can result in a crisis of confidence and a harking back to an era when shanks and other duffed shots were far more common. And if we allow such thoughts to enter our mind, then it's possible that our game will go downhill – at least in the short term.

Muscle memory can be extraordinarily long, especially when it involves shots we no longer wish to play.

The solution? Play a different club for your next shot. Probably one with more loft.

What's vital at this stage is to get back to hitting straight shots again, to recover your swing and to regain your confidence. The consequent lack of distance may mean you take an extra shot on the hole you're playing, but by ensuring you don't adopt the hacker mind set of yesteryear, it could save you several more over the rest of the round.

14. WINNING

WHAT KIND OF a winner are you? And what constitutes a win?

Eeyore Eric

Several years ago, I played two rounds with a golf society at Staverton Park Golf Club in Northamptonshire. In the morning, I arrived on the sixteenth tee with one of my group absolutely incandescent at the golf club for not having a strokesaver available for us to buy at the start of the day.

For the non-golfers amongst us, a strokesaver is a small booklet that is a guide to each hole on the course. It gives you a map of each hole, showing where the hazards are and providing a useful set of distance measurements from the tee and to the hole.

If you haven't played a course before, a strokesaver is the nearest thing you'll get to a caddy, or a knowledgeable and friendly club member.

Anyway, the course didn't have any and when we got to the par-5 fifteenth, Eric's second shot found its way into a tricky fairway bunker that none of us knew existed until we almost fell into it.

Not only had his ball bounced into the bunker, it had managed to roll underneath a lip of turf at the front, making an escape in one shot from its sandy clutches nigh on impossible.

Six shots later, he stormed off the green and onto the sixteenth tee, blaming his lack of knowledge about the bunker for his two out of the sand and his three-putt from eight feet.

With the wind behind him and still doing a decent vocal impression of Muttley from *Wacky Races*, he took out his nine iron, smacked the ball in the direction of the par-3 green and then watched as amazed as any of us as the ball landed on the green, rolled forward eight feet and dropped into the hole 160 yards away.

Cue exuberant celebrations all round with one exception – the man who'd hit the ball.

Eric's mood robbed him of any joy. He just reflected on the bitter irony that the eagle didn't make up for the triple bogey on the previous hole, plus it would probably cost him around forty pounds in drinks later on. In fact, the drinks cost him fifty-six pounds. De Vere hotels are not known for their cheap prices.

What was even more stunning to my playing group was when he put the ball down on the tee for the next hole.

"Surely you're going to keep it… I'd write the date and the course on it and mount it… You might lose it," were answered with "No, it's a golf ball… I'm not interested in your sexual proclivities… I will undoubtedly lose it; that's what happens with every golf ball I have ever owned."

Eric's not good with success. He gets embarrassed when praised. To him, success is never good enough. It could always be better. He recognises the achievement for a nanosecond, then looks to move on.

That's why he played the same ball on the seventeenth and eighteenth that morning and on the first in the afternoon. It didn't make the second tee however. A huge post-lunch slice on the first took it over an equally huge net where it rolled to an anonymous halt amidst six hundred balls on the adjoining practice range.

We were all for ripping down the net, risking the wrath of the golf club and going in search of the ball, but he'd have none of it. The ball had done its job and could now bask in glorious anonymity, free of the pressure of finding the hole with every par-3 tee shot.

Incidentally, in the afternoon round he parred 15, then birdied 16 – leaving him at level par on those two holes over the day. Finally, he was at peace with the course.

It didn't win him the day, which was a relief to all of us, as we didn't have to sit through the most miserable winner's speech ever.

It'd be fair to say that Eric is at one end of the winning spectrum. Tom is at the other.

Tigger Tom

To Tom, every single shot he takes on the golf course is an opportunity to celebrate a victory – either over the ball's lie, the course, the weather, the plane flying overhead or the nearby motorway traffic.

It's impossible for him to take one positive thought off the golf course; he takes dozens of them, if not hundreds.

And he likes to talk about his successes. A lot.

To Tom, there is nobody else on the golf course. Nobody else does anything worthy of note, comment or praise. Reflecting on the round over a pint in the bar turns into a blow-by-blow account of Tom's day on the course. It is possible to get a word in every now and then while he takes a breath, but the conversation soon drifts back to Tom's game.

Poor sap: "It was good to get out on the course again today. Since my wife left me with the kids after I lost my job, my confidence has been shot to pieces and my health has taken a dive. Being out there today was the first time I'd relaxed in weeks, even though I didn't play well. I think my depression is lifting; my life is turning again for the better."

Tom: "Yeah. My greenside bunker shot on the first really got my round going. I couldn't believe I managed to get the check I wanted on the ball – not from that lie."

There isn't even any respite if you get him back on the course. He simply spends the time between making new memories by revisiting old ones.

The thing with Tom is he doesn't gloat if he actually wins. In fact, it's difficult to get anything out of him when he wins. It's as if he hasn't the words to express what it means to him.

Bearing in mind he can turn a six-inch tap-in into a story akin to conquering Everest on one leg, the vastness of winning in matchplay or the enormity of beating the entire field is too big for him to comprehend, never mind appreciate.

To Tom, everything is a win, apart from the win itself. And that's not a bad thing, even if Tom would be a far better golfing partner if he toned things down a bit.

The course has ears and sharp teeth

So, where do you sit on the winning spectrum? Is winning nothing to you, or is it everything?

Does the prospect add a tremor to your putting stroke, or does it put ten yards on your drive?

How does winning (in whatever form) make you feel? Elated? Satisfied? Smug? Cheerful? And how long does that feeling last? Do you hang on to the memory, using it to cheer yourself up in darker, non-golfing times, or do you let it go to make space for new ones?

Are you magnanimous in victory and only talk about it when prompted, or do you laud it over the vanquished every time you meet up, reminding them of the moment even when they have subsequently secured their revenge – because they undoubtedly will.

And what is winning anyway? Does it have to be a victory over an individual or the entire field, or can it be as simple as a great recovery shot, a good putt or just getting round the course without getting wet?

The classic Kipling line "If you can meet with triumph and disaster, and treat those two imposters just the same…" could have been written with golf in mind – and not just about winning or losing in competition.

We all know that however good our game at a specific moment in time and however much we feel we are dominating the course, the course can bite back. And bite hard.

That's why nobody with any sense will tempt fate during the round by mentioning how well they're playing, or how their playing group looks as if it will miss the surrounding rain. Because as soon as you do, the listening golfing gods will take umbrage at your temerity and will ensure the quality of your day rapidly takes a turn for the worse.

Previously straight tee shots will fade into trees, nestling just behind or just in front of the largest trunk in the copse. Straight-as-a-die fairway shots will finish in un-repaired divots.

Nailed-on approach shots will take an inexplicable bounce into the nearest bunker, where they'll end up in an un-raked footprint. Guaranteed tap-ins will horseshoe around the hole before rolling three feet away, from where you will miss your next shot.

The wind will pick up, the sky will darken and the rain will be unleashed with a ferocity last witnessed just as Noah closed the Ark's door, battened down the hatches, put the kettle on and settled in front of the telly for a few weeks.

"Go on then," the course will murmur, so quietly that only you can hear it. "Let's see how good you look at the end of this round."

So, however you're winning, win graciously. Accept the praise of others for a great shot or a dramatic victory with a quiet "thank you" and offer fulsome praise when due in return. Praise the quality of the course; talk with respect about the challenge it presents; comment on how lucky you've been so far with the weather.

Follow this maxim and maybe – just maybe – the course will leave you alone.

The fourteenth hole at our club is a very long par four with a kink two-thirds down the fairway where it passes some woods on the right. For several years after we first joined the club, a friend of mine found these trees with his second shot with monotonous regularity – so much so that we renamed the woods in his honour.

Playing alongside him a couple of years ago, his second shot had successfully negotiated the kink and rested in the middle of the fairway some 80 yards from the pin. "We're going to have to rename that wood," he laughed, as he pulled out his pitching wedge.

A few moments later his ball clattered into the trees, following a horrendous 90-degree shank.

You have been warned. Approach 'winning' with caution.

15. PRESSURE

PRESSURE CERTAINLY PLAYS its part in golf. Whatever the reason for the pressure you feel – a hole to halve the match, a putt to win it, a shot you're not particularly good at, bragging rights in the clubhouse – the source is always the same: you.

Pressure isn't necessarily a bad thing. It can focus the mind, reinforce your determination to do well, calm you down and add a deliberation to every swing you make. The results of taking that pressure and transforming it into something positive can be pretty spectacular. Similarly spectacular can be the crumbling of your game if you can't handle the situation.

Worst of all is when you don't cope with pressure particularly well, but you still actively seek it out in the most innocuous of circumstances.

One time on one of our social golfing trips abroad, I happened to be the only one in my fourball to buy a strokesaver at the clubhouse of a course we'd never played before.

In the spirit of the social occasion and trying to be helpful, I offered guidance to the hazards lying in wait at the start of every hole: "There's a lateral hazard on the left hand edge of the fairway… there's a pond just after the woods on the right... watch out for the ditch crossing in front of the green... back of the green is out of bounds," and so on.

One of the problems for one of my playing partners was that, as soon as he was made aware of a potential issue on the hole, his ball invariably found it. There didn't seem to be a bunker on the course that he didn't visit or a ditch that his ball didn't dive into.

His other problem was that, although he felt my friendly advice was the cause of his misfortune, he didn't ask me to stop giving it. So, every time I opened my mouth, he managed to get it into his head that I was jinxing his shots – providing unhelpful targets that he couldn't help but invariably hit, even though he wasn't aiming for them.

Instead of focusing on getting his game back on track, he found himself waiting for my subtle instruction and would then expect the ball to do what I had suggested. Every time it did, it reinforced his belief in my evil machinations.

The perverse pleasure he got out of this chain of events was unknown to anyone except himself, until that night in the bar, when his account of what had gone so horribly wrong during the day pointed the blame in one direction – mine.

Nobody laughed in disbelief. The groups for the next day were drawn and my three partners turned and made me promise not to offer them any help during our round. There wasn't one smile on their faces.

They were deadly serious - at least, they were until the fourth hole of the next round, by which time they were pleading for some help on the strange course.

There were no other similar incidents over the rest of the holiday, but - to my delight - the issue wasn't forgotten. Even now, many years later, it amuses me to watch the reactions on the tee when I say, "Watch out for the water on the right."

And since then, I have discovered an equally satisfactory method of reducing potential golfing gods to mere mortals with just three simple words – "You're playing well."

Again, it started with the best of intentions, simply offering praise for a playing partner who was putting together an excellent round. But the consequence of my attempts at encouragement - a rapid slide downhill.

You start to split your golfing mates into two groups – those who thrive on pressure and those who do the opposite.

Say "You're playing well," to one golfer and they'll thank you for the compliment and get on with the game, boosted by the respect you have shown and the praise you have given.

Repeat the sentence to a second – or even look at them as if you're about to say it (and they know you're going to say it as they know they're playing well) – and they'll ask you not to say anything. The thought, however, remains with them and they still go to pieces.

The lovely swing

I understand how praise can cause pressure, because it happened to me.

Playing at Pinhal in the Algarve, a pal and I were paired up with a lovely middle-aged couple from England who were coming to the end of their holiday. The atmosphere was exceptionally cordial, the weather was fine, the course was excellent and we were all having a good round.

All was going well, until we reached the tenth tee. Having

crashed a drive down the middle of the fairway, I wandered over to Bill and Alice and waited for my partner to tee off.

"I was just saying to Bill," whispered Alice, "You've got such a lovely swing."

Bill nodded in agreement.

"Thank you very much," I replied.

"It's very relaxed and rhythmical," she murmured, "We could watch it all day."

Unsure if this conversation was going to lead to a proposal for a threesome later on, and totally uncomfortable with praise of any kind, I brought the topic to a close with a quick "Years of practice and clean living…" and dived into my buggy where I was finally joined by my mate. Off we went into the pine trees to look for his wayward slice.

I hadn't really given a great deal of thought to my swing. It had just evolved over the years and really was no better or any worse than those of golfers around me.

Over a decade before Kettering's own Charley Hull had been born, I had followed the mantra she was to voice in her first year or two as a professional: "I hit the ball. I find it. I hit it again."

If you had asked me to analyse my physical swing process or the mental build up to each shot, I wouldn't have had a clue. But, although I still didn't realise it, this unexpected compliment had raised the twin spectres of technique and self-appraisal into my thought process. The results weren't pretty.

Things were fine for the rest of that hole. I didn't have much of an audience on any shot I took. But once we were on the next tee, I had my new fan club watching on appreciatively. Until then, I hadn't consciously had a swing thought, but now I did.

"I've got a lovely swing," I thought. Then I shanked the drive. The following four shots to the green weren't much better. The more I tried to recover my poise and to justify my fan club's admiration, the more I looked like someone trying to combine the sport of golf with the art of breakdancing while under the influence of alcohol.

Bill and Alice looked shocked and a little embarrassed. The social chitchat of the front nine dissolved into an uncomfortable silence, broken only my playing partner's occasional snigger at the collapse of my game.

I was trying to match the expectations of others, rather than playing my own game.

Eventually I learned that it didn't matter what others thought. If by some miracle my game attracts favourable comments, I thank whoever made them, then flush their praise down the same mental toilet that I use for the derisory laughter and the outright disdain that I'm more used to receiving (my friends can be very harsh).

Then I focus on simply hitting the ball, finding it, and hitting it again.

16. LESSONS FOR LIFE

IF YOU'VE ALREADY scraped the bottom of the barrel searching for reasons to justify to your beloved the amount of time you play golf, then rejoice - here's a new, full barrel that will have them encouraging you to play even more.

For all the self-belief engendered, health benefits achieved, physical attributes developed and social skills enhanced by taking up golf, there are also some real life lessons to be learned from this great game.

Any of these can turn you into a better, more whole person, leading a more fulfilling life and improving the lives of those around you as a result. To achieve Nirvana on the fairways takes time, you can explain to your partner, but they will share the benefits resulting from your efforts and investment.

If they think it's just an excuse to play more golf (which it is), here are a few pointers to support your proposition.

We'll start with guitar-playing Canadian astronaut Chris Hadfield.

In his fascinating book *An Astronaut's Guide to Life*, Chris says the most important quality for an astronaut – and for anyone who is striving to succeed at anything at all - is competency.

For an astronaut, he says, "Competence means keeping your head in a crisis, sticking with a task even when it seems hopeless and improvising good solutions to tough problems when every second counts. It encompasses ingenuity, determination and being prepared for anything. Astronauts have these qualities not because we're smarter than everyone else… It's because we are taught to view the world – and ourselves – differently… But you don't have to go to space to learn to do that. It's mostly a matter of changing your perspective."

On the planet the vast majority of us call home (well, you never know…), improving your competence means playing golf.

Nobody's final words on their deathbed are "I wish I had worked more," although I would suggest that at least some think "I wish I'd played more golf."

Here's how strolling the fairways helps change your perspective, puts things into context, helps you win respect, makes you feel valued, gives you a greater feeling of wellbeing and turns you into a better spouse, partner, parent, colleague, boss, friend and neighbour.

i. Make peace with imperfection

In the whole history of golf, no player has played the perfect round – not even any of the best golfers in the world. After all, what is the golfing definition of perfection - a level-par round, birdies on every hole, absolute satisfaction with every swing? Playing well enough to beat your competition?

In February 2015, Tiger Woods announced he was taking an indefinite break from the game, having carded an 82 at the Phoenix Open and then withdrawing from the following event, saying he needed "a lot of work" on his game.

The announcement attracted plenty of comment from the great and the good of the golfing world, but perhaps the most relevant was that made by Paul Azinger who said, "What Tiger has done is sacrifice a winning swing at the altar for a quest for the perfect swing. And a perfect swing doesn't exist."

So, if imperfection haunts the best golfers in the world, why should we be any different? We're not perfect – either on or off the golf course, in our work, in our relationships, or with our kids.

It can get to us, either because our failings are pointed out to us (sometimes gleefully, sometimes critically, occasionally by an interminable and uncomfortable silence) or, in an extraordinary physical feat, we manage to get on our own backs and beat ourselves up.

One method of coping with your own failure on or off the course is to adopt a trigger phrase to utter when things don't go according to plan.

It saves the simmering anger, the ongoing self-flagellation, the bitter resentment and the slump into depression. It enables you to get on with the game, with your job, with your life.

The trigger phrase is shorthand for saying:

"You know what? I messed up. I didn't mean to and I didn't want to, but I'm not going to beat myself up about it.

I accept I'm not perfect and that these things will happen.

Hopefully I've learned something positive from the experience and - who knows - maybe I've learned a little bit more about myself. Now I shall put this feeling of disappointment to one side and shall move on."

I use the words "Hey ho." Others can be a little more colourful.

Of course, your golfing friends may get a little exasperated if your innumerable duff shots, missed putts and failed bunker escapes mean they hear the same phrase over and over again.

What will wind them up even more is to see that you're not being wound up. That's why it is sometimes better just to think the words – even if the act of actually saying them serves in part as a useful release valve.

ii Know your limitations

Our annual golf trip abroad involves golfers of all shapes, sizes and abilities. One regular is Kev 'Dinky' Davies – 'Dinky' being an accurate description of how he knocks the ball down the middle of every fairway.

Kev isn't a regular golfer and, getting on in years, is awarded a handicap of 28 for the purposes of these tournaments. On one trip to Spain and in the heat of the early afternoon, Kev's group arrived on the tee of the twelfth hole - a par five - that entailed a diagonal tee shot across a wide and deep ravine onto the fairway beyond.

Three players teed off with various degrees of success. Kev sat in the buggy, fiddling with a Tupperware box.

"Kev, it's your turn," prompted one of his partners. Kev looked up and surveyed the challenge ahead. "No thanks," he replied, waving a sandwich in the air. "I'll eat this instead."

Kev knew that his dinky game would simply land him in trouble at this hole and there was no bale-out option for him.

Some (including one or two already mentioned in this book) would have gone for it believing they were good enough when in fact they weren't. Others would have 'had a go' – with the words themselves suggesting abject failure even before the ball had been struck.

Kev plays the course on his terms. He scores where he can, but he also knows when it's best to step back and leave well alone. He rarely loses a ball or his temper, treats all his shots – good and bad – just the same, and laughs a lot.

And knowing your limitations is even more important off the course than it is on it.

It can be as obvious as knowing the amount you can drink before keeling over or acknowledging you lack the basic ability to undertake a particular task (mine is successful DIY). It may be recognising you'll never have the talent or the influence required to progress at work.

Of course, there may be things you can change to overcome these limitations – taking a course or gaining more qualifications at night school, practicing how to use a drill before turning the wall into a holey (sic) mess, or joining the same cycling club as your line manager. But these only work (a) if you have the time, the cash and the willingness to look a prat in Lycra and (b) if you have the basic potential and the desire and determination to progress.

If you don't, then aspiring to attain certain goals and wasting time, energy and money pursuing them only leads to stress, pressure, strained relationships, misery and failure.

Surely it's much better to accept who you are, to recognise your limits and to build a contented life for yourself and those around you within them.

Why take on something you know is genuinely beyond you? Relax and eat the sandwich.

iii. Why worry about things that have yet to happen?

We've all played with Jonah - the golfer who appears to revel in the misfortune of others to such an extent that they predict failure at every opportunity.

Hit a tee shot with a touch of fade and it will have definitely dropped into the ditch 200 yards away (although nobody could see it). Cream a long approach to a well-guarded green and your ball has definitely rolled into the bunker (even though nobody witnessed it).

Attempting a snap hook around some trees has simply left your ball behind even bigger trees on the other side of the fairway with no shot to the green (even though your ball disappeared into the glare of the late, low sun immediately after you hit it).

And for every Jonah, there's someone in the group who is equally sure the ball is safe, no matter how doomed it looked in flight. "It'll be fine; it's okay," is their soothing mantra, even though your ball has sailed over trees and out of sight on a course none of you have played before.

"How do you know?" you want to scream in their face. "Played here before in another life have we? Using our X-ray vision to see through solid objects? Linking in to your mate on the International Space Station who happens to be watching our game from sixty miles above us through an exceptionally large and powerful pair of binoculars?"

Whichever of these extremes you're faced with, whether you're dealing with Jonah or Mr. Brightside, you have a choice.

You can believe what they say and spend the next minute

or so experiencing emotions of despair or relief that are totally wrong and which ultimately make the transition to relief or despair so much more dramatic than it needed to be.

You can openly disagree with their opinion, spend the next minute or two arguing the toss and ultimately be vindicated or proven completely wrong - either result doing little for the bonhomie of the game and possibly adversely affecting your own performance. Or, recognising the shot has been taken, the ball is where it is irrespective of anyone else's opinion and you'll deal with whatever is facing you once you've reached it, you simply say, "We'll find out when we get there," and proceed with the game.

This is a discipline that really can apply to other parts of your life as well.

Mark Twain perhaps said it best. "I have been through some terrible things in my life, some of which actually happened."

How much time, energy and emotion do we waste, worrying about things that don't ever happen or, if they do, are much less troublesome than we imagined?

When you catch yourself in this kind of situation, simply imagine yourself on a fairway, not knowing whether or not your ball has found a greenside bunker or rolled up to the flag.

Rather than running through all the permutations of predicament and possible response, just say to yourself, "We'll find out when we get there," enjoy the walk and then decide on what to do when you know what you're facing.

It'll save you a lot of stress and won't do your relationship with those around you any harm either.

iv. Become more patient

If you've reached this far into the book, then you are undoubtedly a golfer who, I venture to guess, has lost patience on the course at some stage, either with your own game or someone else's. Probably both.

Whatever the reason for your irritability, it's likely that your game suffered as a result.

I'd like to start by talking about etiquette.

To the majority of golfers, being part of the golfing community means adhering to its rules and showing care and respect, both to the course and to the game's other participants.

This group acceptance of a uniform set of standards helps create a sense of belonging, where all are equal except in the car park where the club president, captains and professional tend to have their own allotted spaces.

If there is one thing likely to cause irritation, a murmur of annoyance, a nervous twitch and even the occasional raised eyebrow on a golf course, it is a lack of etiquette.

This may manifest itself in those players who believe that sound only travels to the edge of their own fairway, then stops – allowing them to chat, laugh, shout and swear with impunity, no matter how close they are to other people trying to play their own game.

It could be golfers who can't be bothered or who are too embarrassed to shout fore even as their ball travels with tremendous speed and unerring accuracy towards a target unaware of his or her impending doom.

Maybe it's those golfers who leave their bag the wrong

side of the green, then insist on writing their score down and cleaning and replacing their club before moving back across the front of the green to the next tee.

Unraked bunkers; divots not replaced; pitchmarks not repaired; a lack of effort to keep up with the group in front; an unwillingness to call the following group through even though three holes have been lost on the group in front – all are guaranteed to create murmurs of discontent in the groups behind.

Sometimes a quiet word on the course or in the bar afterwards is all that it needed to ensure that transgressions are not repeated. A note to the committee can result in helpful reminders being issued to everyone.

Notices can appear in the pro shop and signs on the first tee. Course marshals can be briefed to keep an eye on miscreants and to pull them up using all the authority at their disposal.

Such actions, or a combination of them, play their part in maintaining acceptable levels of etiquette and helping to speed up the pace of the game.

Only slightly down the irritation scale are players – sometimes novices, but many times not – who are well aware of the concept of etiquette, but aren't quite sure what form it takes. So they make up their own.

Their first rule is to be ready to move off promptly after the tee shot, which is why they rattle their driver back into their bag even as their playing partners tee off.

The second rule is to make sure they are following the rules by asking their partners to confirm what they can or cannot do, over and over again – more often than not for the same situation.

Rule three is to speed up play by hitting their ball as soon as they reach it, rather than waiting for those further away to hit first; or to warm up for this next shot by taking practice swings at pine cones as their partners try to concentrate on their own stroke.

Next is to speed up on the green by focusing on their own ball and putting out, even though it means standing on the lines of others still to play. On the rare occasions they remember to tend the flag for their partners, they forget to remove it as the ball trundles towards the hole, waiting instead for the screams of "Take it out! Take it out!" before reacting.

Finally, to aid the scorer (because they never score if they can help it), they'll stand in the middle of the green while the game goes on around them, looking back down the fairway and pointing to where they took their shots, voicelessly mouthing the number of each one until they come up with a final figure and announce "I took seven," right on the downswing of a playing partner's putt.

Whatever the transgression, I used to be the world's worst when reacting to it. If a four-ball in front of my group were obviously slow, I'd feel my blood start to rise – especially if the day was cold and wet. Invariably my next shot wouldn't be great and I'd start examining the miscreants in greater detail.

One of them would leave their bag on the wrong side of the green. Maybe they'd all try to find one player's ball before taking their own shots from the fairway.

Worst of all would be the club cleaning or the card marking by the side of the green they'd just played, rather than at the next tee when they'd be out of range.

89

This lack of consideration for others on the course, this blissful ignorance of golfing etiquette would outrage me. I would grumble about the disgraceful behaviour to my playing partners. It would wind me up – a situation that would not be helped by any future shot in the round that was less than perfect, which would wind me up even more.

If a cardiologist had ever played alongside me and had seen the veins pumping in my neck and my face turning a funny colour, I think she'd have made a discrete phone call to the clubhouse to check the defibrillator was charged up and ready for action.

Sometimes I managed to temper my temper, but occasionally my frustration would get the better of me. I'd never shout, "Get a move on," or anything similar but in stronger, more colourful language.

I'd never deliberately fire a 'hurry up' tee shot that would roll gently past the bemused group and prompt some hard stares from both parties – although, again, I've seen that on the course.

My strategy was, I liked to think, much more subtle.

I'd wait until they were moving on up the fairway or strolling at a funereal pace away from a green, then I'd mutter a "Sorry about this" to my playing partners then – before hitting my shot – would bellow "Fore!" as loud as I could.

The shout would help vent my frustration and the sight of ducking golfers scurrying away from our target area gave me a grim satisfaction. My playing partners would be suitably embarrassed and - once the grim satisfaction has dissipated - so would I.

Crucially, it never helped my game. I would lose focus and

wouldn't be able to recover it.

Interestingly, I didn't consciously change my attitude on the course in order to improve my game.

It came about as an indirect result of the epiphany in Spain that featured earlier.

I didn't even know my attitude had changed until I noticed some playing partners complaining about the group in front. I hadn't even realised there was a problem. I wasn't looking for negatives on the golf course, I was too busy appreciating the positives.

And when I did notice delays in front, I found myself looking to excuse the actions of the guilty party. They were slow - but everyone has their own pace. They were hackers - but so were we when we started off. They traipsed back over the green to grab a bag they'd left on the wrong side - but we all make mistakes.

Learning the art of patience can also have an impact across other elements of your life. Railing against the incompetence of others simply raises your own blood pressure, puts you in a bad mood and risks confrontations that could make things much worse.

Drivers up your backside on the motorway may be in a genuine hurry, could well be shortsighted and will probably die before you do – as long as you let them past in their rush to their own doom and keep focused on your own safety and that of your passengers.

Slow cars in front of you may contain drivers of a nervous disposition, who may panic if pressured and create catastrophe as a result. Best to keep your distance and your patience, overtaking only when it is safe to do so.

There's nothing quite so galling as being pulled over by the local constabulary following a few seconds' speeding to overtake a slow-moving vehicle, only to see the reason for your downfall toddle past, frowning in concentration and oblivious to all as they focus on the road in front of them. Believe me. I know.

Similarly, losing patience for whatever reason at home can also be tantamount to disaster of one form or another. So what if you need to wait another ten minutes for the bathroom, or *Coronation Street* runs across the first fifteen minutes of the football?

Take a step back and be grateful for the people around you and the joy they generally bring to your life. It'll make you happier and your life much easier.

v. Accept it: life isn't fair

I think the most spectacular shot I have hit in golf was a 190-yard four iron that looked as if it was going to bounce just before the green and roll up towards the pin.

It certainly bounced. It landed on the front edge of a sprinkler head and rebounded fifty yards back and left, where it ricocheted forward off one rock onto another, which propelled it skywards and backwards once more, into a waiting lake.

It beats the 240-yard downhill drive on a shortish par four that managed to hit the cart path crossing the fairway and bounced impressively over the green, the back bunker and the bushes that marked the limit of the course and the edge of the car park.

Maybe it doesn't quite beat a friend of mine who, for a time, had all the golfing luck in the world.

Slieve Russell is an excellent course on the southern side of the Irish border. A long par three on the back nine has water to the front and the right of a raised green, which is well defended by bunkers. Access to the green is over a bridge slightly to the left, which crosses the wide stream that feeds into the large pond. The bridge's three-foot high walls are made of rough, angular brickwork, without a straight edge to be seen.

It's a tough tee shot, which my mate made even tougher by hooking his fairway wood left. Being the competitive sort, and being one down at the time, my heart leapt and I looked on expectantly.

The ball arced towards the bridge, bounced off the left

hand wall towards the right hand wall, pinged off there back to the left hand wall and rocketed over the bridge, between two bunkers and into the heart of the green, where it settled a yard from the pin.

In each of the above cases, to a greater or lesser extent, I was disappointed and despondent. In each case, the quality of the shot had not ended with the result it deserved. In each case, things hadn't worked out in my favour.

It's a fact. Golf isn't fair. Those who reckon everything evens out are self-deluded. But it doesn't matter whether you get the rub of the green – that's out of your hands. What matters is how you deal with the outcome of the injustice.

In the above cases, the answer is 'not very well'. It put me off my game. Every subsequent poor shot just served to remind me how unfair the game was and how it seemed to be set against me. It almost got to the stage where I was actually looking for the next piece of misfortune to reinforce this belief.

There was almost a grim satisfaction in seeing the ball scuttle across the floor when it should have sailed through the air, or nestle in a bunker when it should have plopped onto the green.

Similar experiences in life will see someone bump into your brand new car, or pull out of buying your house, or be given credit for work that you were involved in. The final result of your winning six-bet accumulator will be changed by a goal in the dying seconds, leaving you with nothing.

The week you forget to buy your lottery tickets will be the week you would have won some cash. You'll have forgotten to record your favourite television show the week of the climax that's been building for ages – and it isn't on catch-up.

Whatever the problem, take a step back and try to put things in perspective. Nobody has the perfect life (like nobody has the perfect game), so you were probably half-expecting something to happen anyway; you just didn't know what or when.

Now that it's arrived, ask yourself "Will this matter a day, month or year from now?" Nine hundred and ninety-nine times out of one thousand, the answer will be no. And if that's the case, put what's happened down to experience, see it as yet another pulled thread in life's rich tapestry, look for lessons to be learned then forget about it and get on with the game.

vi. Give what you'd like to receive

It may be a generalisation, but I reckon it's a pretty accurate one. We all want to feel appreciated, to be respected and to be liked.

With the exception of hermits, we all like to experience the safety and security that is part of being in a close community – although it's possible that hermits themselves like to feel part of the community of hermits, even though they don't know who the other members are or where they live.

That's partly why we're members of a golf club, why we tend to play with the same group of golfers and why most of us quite like the sociability of the clubhouse, where we know people (some of whom we've never played with) and they know us.

Mutual recognition, friendly acknowledgement and informal greetings make us feel an important part of a larger society. We feel valued.

Of course, basking in the warm community glow doesn't come without effort. A community's members communicate with each other. Reputations are built on how others see you. In a golf club, that tends to be based on your behaviour in the clubhouse and on the course.

But we all know how savage a game of golf can be; how it can strip away your protective social layers and lay bare your very soul to those witnesses around you.

As has been suggested more than once in this book, it isn't what *happens* to you on a golf course that is key; it's how you *react* and *respond* to it.

Hooking two consecutive drives out of bounds can happen to the best of us and may be the focus of a couple of asides over a pint or two later on. But if your reaction to the second shot was to throw your club, or to slam it into the sacred turf that is the tee, accompanied by a volley of expletives, or to storm off in a huff?

That is where unwelcome reputations are made.

Behaviour on the course makes you somebody other golfers want to play with, have to tolerate or deliberately avoid. And it isn't just your behaviour in relation to your own game that is important. Equally important is how you react and respond to your playing partners and to other people on the course.

Basically, if you would like to be well regarded (and who wouldn't), then give what you'd like to receive.

If you would like good shots to be recognised as such, then be fulsome in your praise of the good shots of others. If somebody is struggling, be quick to encourage them.

If your opponent's hooked tee shot gets a lucky rebound that finishes in position A, then congratulate them on their good fortune and hope the next bit of luck comes your way.

Practice humility. Nobody likes bombast. If someone praises your game, either on the course or in the bar afterwards, a simple "thank you" will do rather than launching into a detailed account of what happened for the benefit of those who didn't have the dubious privilege of being there at the time.

Resist the urge to criticise or gloat. Neither will win you friends. Criticism doesn't benefit anyone or anything apart from your superiority complex. Gloating may provide short-term solace, especially in a sport where, as already discussed, the course has a way of biting back and biting hard.

And if you're the subject of criticism, don't fight it, don't argue and don't try to explain. Agree with it. Then watch it fade away.

Similarly, don't react to gloating, at all. Ignore it completely. Neither criticism nor gloating can operate in a vacuum. If you don't respond the way you're expected to respond, there's nothing for the protagonist to feed on.

The social protocols behind our upbringing mean we are used to reacting or responding to anything and everything that is thrown at us, but there's no rule that says we have to.

Remember, in life as well as golf, if someone throws you a ball, you don't have to catch it - although it may be advisable to dodge swiftly if it's heading for your face.

17. THE KEY POINTS

WE ALL KNOW what happens if you stand over your ball with too many thoughts in your head. That's why this is only a short guide!

Hopefully there is enough food for thought in its pages to help you to see the game in a different light and to come off the course all the better for having stepped onto it in the first place.

Here's a reminder of the key points:

Golf is a teacher. It's a live-fire exercise, designed to instill attitudes that help you to get the most out of your day-to-day existence, as well as your game.

Golf is all about enjoying yourself, relishing the challenges and your achievement in overcoming them and creating warm memories.

List everything you like about playing golf and build a greater appreciation of your time on the course.

Remember and accept that the course giveth and the course taketh away.

Practice your short game.

Make sure you are in the right frame of mind to execute whatever shot is required - maintain a positive but realistic mindset.

Turn problems into opportunities; find the extraordinary in the ordinary.

The better we think we are, the greater the expectation and the bigger the pressure. Use a release valve to get rid of the pressure.

Don't rely on a go-to club.

If you shank a shot, use a club with a bit more loft for the next one.

Never tempt fate during the round; the course will bite back.

Perfection doesn't exist. Savour the times you get close.

Keep things simple. Hit the ball, find it, then hit it again.

Don't strive for goals that are way outside your capabilities. Sometimes it's better just to eat the sandwich.

Don't waste time worrying about things that may not happen.

Enjoy the walk.

Whatever the problem, take a step back and try to put things in perspective. Will it matter a year from now?

It isn't what happens to you that is important; it's how you react and respond to it.

Don't expect to absorb everything, but if any of these points strike a chord, then that can only be good news for you, for those around you and for your game.

You'll be well on your way to becoming a true golf guru. Now, get back on the course and put it all into practice!

THE AUTHOR

PHIL RENNETT WAS born in Warrington, England and now lives in Rugby with partner Clare, Molly the rescued greyhound, a ginger cat and several fish.

He took up golf in his early thirties following a sports-related injury that cut short his days playing hockey, soccer, cricket and squash.

For twenty years or so, he has thrashed his way around golf courses the length and breadth of the UK and across Europe.

He spends most of his time away from the course trying to persuade Clare he should spend more time on it.

This book is his latest and best attempt to date.

NOTE FROM THE AUTHOR

Thank you for reading *You! A Golf Guru!*

I hope you have enjoyed it and that you're taking away some ideas to help you get more out of your game.

If you have found the book helpful, please consider leaving a rating and review on your preferred book retailer site or praising it to the heavens in your clubhouse (after you've secured the free drinks mentioned much earlier, of course).

Finally, I'd be interested in hearing about your own experiences on the golf course.

If you've any you'd like to share, or if you'd like to keep up-to-date with my own golfing journey, please visit

www.youagolfguru.com

This book is dedicated to the memory of

Julie Grimes

Julie was wonderful, bright and funny lady and an extremely talented artist who had just started to forge an exciting new career for herself creating eye-catching portraits of people and animals in her own unique, inimitable style.

We had just started to work on the initial concepts for this book's cover design when she became ill.

Less than four weeks later, she passed away.

Rest In Peace, Julie.

We miss you.

Printed in Great Britain
by Amazon.co.uk, Ltd.,
Marston Gate.